No School Tie

Peter Phillips

Ward Wood Publishing
www.wardwoodpublishing.co.uk

Published by Ward Wood Publishing
6 The Drive
Golders Green
London NW11 9SR
www.wardwoodpublishing.co.uk

The right of Peter Phillips to be identified as author of
this work has been asserted by him in accordance with
the Copyright, Designs and Patent Act, 1988.
Copyright © 2011 Peter Phillips
ISBN: 978-0-9568969-0-2
British Library Cataloguing in Publication Data. A CIP
record for this book can be obtained from the British
Library.

Designed and typeset in Palatino Linotype by
Ward Wood Publishing.
Cover design by Mike Fortune-Wood.
Artwork: Boy On Tracks by Rimzphoto.
Supplied by agency: Dreamstime.

Printed and bound in Great Britain by
Imprint Digital, Seychelles Farm,
Upton Pyne, Exeter EX5 5HY, UK

*In memory of Linda Phillips
and for my family*

Acknowledgements

Some of these poems, or versions of them, first appeared in:
14 Magazine, Acumen, Assent, Brittle Star, Ham & High, Hampstead Garden Suburb Centenary Brochure, Morning Star, N2 Poetry, Orbis International, Rialto, Smiths Knoll, South Bank Poetry, Suburb News, The Interpreter's House, The Spectator, Weyfarers.

'Faith in Flowers' was commissioned in 2007 by The Hampstead Garden Suburb Residents' Association to celebrate the Suburb's centenary.

Contents

III NO SCHOOL TIE

No School Tie

I

TWINS

For Arthur and Daisy

Generations

To my first wife

The clock in my head strikes
back to your death.
Our daughter is having twins.
Will you hear them cry?

To my daughter

They must be having fun
in the bright cave
of your stomach.
You are all lit up.

To my grandchildren

I can see you in that cramped space
looking out for each other,
feeling the certainty
of your mother's heart.

Birth Day

Dashed to delivery through empty streets
before the day's noise and sun had risen.

The knife made its cut. You were lifted out,
10 lbs of twins, to the sound of Magic FM,

doctor and midwife swapping Saturday night
stories of missed love and kisses; then into

your mother's arms at the edge of your first day.

                           *

You lie in the cot, heads touching
in your two-week earliness.

I listen to the silence of new-born breath.

It's 2am

I carry you downstairs,
offer warm milk. Your head

rests on my arm – no
binge drinker like your brother,

you take the bottle, suckling
gently in sleep.

I pat your back. You repay me
with a genteel burp,

after all, you are my granddaughter

Companionship

You smile at your brother,
reach and touch his face.

He doesn't pull away. Maybe
he senses the darkness

when four legs kicking
and a sideways prod meant

he wasn't the only one there.
He rolls onto his front, stares

at your face as if you and he
are nothing to each other.

Their Cries

Her cry is lighter, not as wretched
as his. She takes longer
to start, quiet tremble,
look of pity, then
a weightless scream.

He lets us know the world
owes him milk. A battle cry
does the job, no messing about
with the delicate stuff.

When You Woke

I lifted you from the cot;
your brother slumbered on.

You stopped crying, lay
between us in our bed.

Blue eyes dark in the morning gloom
arms outstretched, looking

at your hands. Then three fingers
in your mouth. Today

you've gone home. I
can still see your eyes.

Granddaughter

She doesn't seem to mind
him taking the biscuit from her hand;

touches my face with a gentle pat,
aware there will always be enough food;

holds the bottle delicately, drinks
from the beaker without spluttering;

knows if she puts a muslin
over her head, I'll laugh.

Grandson

His right eyebrow quivers to a frown.
It's only me, grandson, I understand

your reserve, it's so easy to inherit.
Don't worry, four months is still

very young. Come, sit on my lap.
Now you smile shy and warm.

That's better, I knew you could.

At the Swimming Baths

She'll be easier than him, my daughter says. *You take
her,* a wet package delivered into my hands.

I place her on a towel, on my jacket on the baby changer,
amongst the shouts from local lads, bang of locker doors.

She looks at me. I pat her dry, mismanage her nappy,
take it off, put it on the right way, then trousers and top.

I'm still chatting but she can't manage a smile. Wet,
I dress with one hand and two eyes on her. It's done.

I carry her to reception. We sit in quiet exhaustion.

Dreamland Pleasure Ride

Along the air's wide slopes, over
the park's swings, their scooters rise

then, like on a big dipper, plunge
to land in a pool of laughter. I wish

those long gone could feel
the happiness and splashing water –

she flicking hair from her face, him calling
wait, wait as he hoists his trousers – and they're

off on their Dreamland pleasure ride, soaring
round the park. After lunch, they ask for a story,

a dance, muslins to go to sleep on and would not
have stirred till... who knows when, if their mother

surprised at the quiet, had not woken them.

A Place to Have Babies

When I walk you through Crouch End
everywhere there are babies,

a harvest of twins even.
Mothers with twins smile at me.

I don't mind if they do.
Do they think you're mine?

Buggies are like lawn mowers,
supermarket trolleys. But where

is the Silver Cross pram, the thrum
of its engine as it glides past?

And where's the Norland nanny,
her starched uniform ironed into place,

or young au pairs wobbling along
with cigarettes in their mouths?

Battalions from the silver brigade
puff about, hunched over prams.

I'm looking at babies.
Can this really be me?

It Started with Socks

Somewhere in the world are your missing
socks, the ones you pull off in

moments of boredom, that get stuck down
the side of the buggy, sofa, toy box.

Maybe you've invented a 'Let's
see how many socks we can lose' game:

the blue ones with the grey stripes,
or pink with white stars, the plain

navy or reds with orange heels. Today
you've started to take off your shoes, nearly

lost one sandal in Budgens, another
at the library. Trailing behind us

are your socks. If anyone frowns at your feet
will I have to say something?

Present from Woolworths

Two hours dismantling errors,
squinting at instructions

as concentration slides
through my fingers, building the swing.

It's ready. I stand back
amazed, want to climb in.

In he goes. The motion of a first
push moves him, his face is a blur.

A wide-angle smile focuses.
He's away.

Playgroup Leader

The twins are in my lap. Kate
changes the music, a Queen anthem
thumps out. She turns, hands held
towards us, asks *Would you like to dance?*
and I'm thinking, 'Yes, I would.'

She's like my first wife, hair dropping down
her shoulders. *Come on* she says
with a smile, but grandson holds onto me.
Off she goes, opening
her arms to Owen, another two-year-old,

who jumps up. They twirl round. Lucky boy.

Rest Time

I put them into sleeping bags, fumble
with the zip, get my glasses, try again,
am stopped by their faces:

his hair, curling round his ears
like blond question marks, eyes
a shade of blue exclamation closing

slightly as he smiles goodbye. She
gives a sleepy grin, wider than I deserve.
Even though her mother says she smiles a lot,

it makes me think she likes me. I go
downstairs, lie back in the chair,
close my eye

Going Dry

No nappies today
but this dry run turns out
not to be. Oh dear.
Five *episodes*.
Is that too delicate a word?
It is, but in another twenty
years it might be me.
So I'll be polite.

II

CONVERSATIONS

I Did Say It

You really think that? she said.

No I didn't mean that,
not that.

But you did say it, didn't you?

Yes I did say it –
It was just…

*Then that was a particularly
unpleasant thing to say.*

But I didn't really mean it,
I just didn't express…

You did say it?

Yes I did.

Well then…

Look, you know I did,
I've told you I did
and now
I feel like saying it again.

Janek's Story

The landlord, is it right, 'landlord'?
He give me one room for Ania and baby.
Landlord say his grandfather come also Poland,
six sleep in one room.

I say I want two rooms,
soon baby be big. Westminster say
I soon get two rooms.
Landlord get loud, angry.

I say I know rights, me and Ania and baby
need two rooms. He get more loud,
say bad names, things. I know I immigrant.
I say, I immigrant.

But his family also immigrant out from Poland?
He say they had no rights.
I say his family make use of rights if have them?
He say I not work, Westminster pay rent.

I work. Some English no work –
smoke, drink. I pay, what you say, tax?
I do work for small money.
I say grandfather fly for England in war.

He stop. He red in face. He say
ok Janek you have two rooms.

It Was Your Light

that drew me to you. Light
in my arms, our first dance.

And the first kiss, me wanting to,
you letting me. But twenty years ago

a winter wind found you
and blew and blew.

The Acer Tree

We saw it learn to dance
then pirouette and arabesque
bloom into leaf as it grew,

thirty years from a wisp of air
into a ballerina, branches
picking up light and grace in the breeze.

Now it sways in the garden,
rhythmically shading the lawn,
reminding me of you.

Forgetfulness

It happens. Mother died of it, the name a terrier's
spiteful bite. When it's my time, I hope
to remember what a medium rare steak is,

get excited by white flakes of beer battered fish.
If you see me dreamy in a pub, a pint sitting
patiently by my hand, come up and say,

Hello, Peter, fancy some fish and chips?
Then raise a glass of London Pride
(imaginary if you like). That will be enough

to jolt me back. Hopefully, I won't have been
too far, just to the edge of the plate.

Faith in Flowers

(A Hampstead Garden Suburb centenary poem)

What did you say, dear?
One hundred years, Henrietta.
Wouldn't you like to be there?
I can't think that far,
with so much to do tomorrow.
Yes, yes, I know Mr Parker and Mr Unwin
will be dead – and so will we.

Did I tell you – please listen Samuel
and do remember to rest –
I asked them what flowers they enjoyed?
Mr Unwin said daffodils and Mr Parker crocuses.
I said I hoped to plant some bulbs
in our Central Square

and would try to ensure
they'd be set out
in beautiful order and symmetry,
just like their houses. Then I saw
them glance at each other and smile.
Could I have made them smile, dear husband?

But wouldn't you like to be there –
see all your fruit trees?
No. It's one thing to have a life's duty
quite another to go back when one's dead...
The world does so hurry along,
and I couldn't endure that.

But I know our architects' flowers will flourish –
crocuses gossiping like schoolgirls,
daffodils caring for them –
so much colour
as our churches hum to the hymn of Easter.
Do you think Mr Parker and Mr Unwin
would be pleased with that?

In 1907 Dame Henrietta Barnet and her husband, The Canon Samuel Barnet, founded Hampstead Garden Suburb, now a renowned conservation area in North London.

Giraffe in Hampstead Garden Suburb

A giraffe glides through Central Square, thinks *Where's
Regents Park, the canal-side morning view?* She reaches

to munch a hedge, spreads her wigwam legs to prod
a tennis ball, stares at the long-necked Lutyens spire.

*But where are the chugging barges, the man with bananas
and hay?* Across Meadway into Heathgate, down

the steps in one gangly stride. *Where's that fragrant
casserole of smells: elephant, tiger, reptile, wolf?*

She snuffles the breeze, treads lightly through the daffodils
onto the Heath, nods at the Superintendent.

Cathy on the Beach

She's got a bottle between her knees,
straining to get the cork out.
I plunge in, swim around,
am pulled under.
I come up. She waves,
smiles one of her smiles,
holds up the bottle and a glass.
I go down and I'm thinking
Cathy's watching me drown.
I come up. She's still waving.
I don't splash or shout.
My mouth fills with water.
I go under for a third time,
know I might not come up.

Looking for a Drink

You have a knack of finding good places
for us to stop for a drink. You see an inviting
sign or an outside table with a view –

an offer I, not wanting to cross the road,
can't help nidgying at. We go there anyway.
I have a cold beer. You moan at me for

being miserable, tell me I should have
more faith. So I say you've got enough
for both of us, and you smile

from the faint lines around your eyes.

A City Boy Trader Said to Me

Every December I value my house
then the place in Tuscany, tot up the closing
prices in the FT, add in the value of my Ferrari.

I said, 'Do you have a strong sense of worth?'
What do you mean? he asked,
looking at me, perhaps thinking
it might be a trick question.

'How do you value yourself?' I said.
Oh, he replied,
I thought you were having a pop at me.
Lots of friends and family are.

He finished his glass of red, grabbed
another from a floating tray
and began to smoke a cheese straw.

'What is Wall Street, Daddy?'

is a question your daughter may ask one day,
but today is no day for an answer. Maybe one Fall
when the dollar, tired and shamed, stops fluttering
like the golden leaf it used to be, you'll say

That is where it all finished darling. She'll remember
that photograph (you carrying your box of belongings)
the one flushed round the world like something dirty
and will hold even tighter to the money in her pocket.

Remembrance

We all knew it was dangerous
but they wanted you to go. Information,
always information... Beirut was a long way.

They said I should meet him in a bar.
I think they chose me
because I looked innocent.

I liked him straight away.
He was five years older than me.
His face wasn't handsome.

We chatted a little at first,
pleasantries. I was drinking soda water,
and he ordered two white wines
without asking. I liked that.

I felt a different person.
It's not me, I heard myself say,
and when he touched my hand
I knew it was necessary
but part of me wanted to.

Before we'd left the bar, I managed to get most
of what they wanted. Mother always told me
not to be greedy. I still never choose
the most expensive dish on the menu.
Besides, I wanted to live.

We went to bed.
Everything opened... better than my first time,
and he did it again.
He said we should meet after the war.
I knew they were words.
He'd be about ninety now.

Andrei Kushkov

I answer box in *Postcard Monthly*, ten years go.
I write, say I send religion cards, cards of synagogues.
He write me quick, say he pay price cards he like.

I ask he send dollars to Olga, Helsinki –
no letter sent here, St Petersburg. We no speak.
I register cards. He register dollars.

Ten, twelve letters year I sending. He pay Olga
for stamps also. Olga my girl… girlfriend you say?
She have yellow hair down back. She my bank,

my pretty bank! I visit Olga, we go bars. We drink
red wine to Mister Fineman. I sending cards,
he sending dollars. We drink, laugh, do much love.

Mister Fineman happy. He pay quick always.
I pay kopeks, he pay dollars. I much happy –
Olga best bank in Helsinki.

Lisa

My five-year-old broke his arm.
It'd have been quicker to take him to Cromer,
but they'd closed the x-ray department –
so we went to the big hospital at Lynn.
You can't stop them playing around,
he's a double handful.

But he's better off than we were.
I used to play in the fields,
the church grounds and round
the back of the pub. My mum
never knew where I was.
I realize that now.

We've got two babysitters and two cars;
that means I can do taxiing at weekends.
I like trying to find the quickest way,
doing the back lanes.
There's two main drives to Holt,
but I've found another three.
I love seeing the owls, sitting
in their white coats.
They've got yellow eyes
and their faces seem kind.
They swoop at the last minute.

I know I was a bit wild
but I think I've turned out alright.
I'll drop you here.
That's five pounds fifty please.

Snow Falls in Ghostly Flurries

An owl sits on the road. His white coat
shines in the headlamps. He's
the wisest owl I've ever seen

or wanted to be. I get out, ask
Are owls anxious birds?
I reach, touch his head and stroke

his armoured wings. He lets me have this gift.
Then the owl inside me rises up and over
the hedgerow into a wisdom of thoughts.

Norfolk Lament

Light – tattered seams
        creep over marshes
                enlighten like a hymn

Lace – delicate from waves
        decorate the sand
                insistent like a prayer

Breath – silhouette
        of winter coming in
                mournful like regret

Whisper – a hint of the past
        intimate heat
                a touch in the night

The Horse

A train munches through the valley, eating
Devon countryside in large mouthfuls. Golden
nuggets of gorse are smothered by steam,

flare up as the clatter dies away. The horse,
wild in its fury, kicks the ground. If there were
words he'd swear. He shakes his head, snorts

as if to say *This is my land.* Later another
rumbles past, showering gritty vapour.
His eyes blink. He lowers his head to a stream,

refreshes his throat and the trains keep coming.
The horse broods, the way horses do
in that brown flank sort of way,

swishes his tail, gallops up and over
stubbled ground of the moor, towards
the one he hopes will understand.

His nostrils breathe cold wind. All he smells
is burning cinder. He turns and turns.
Where is she? His eyes are still smarting.

Three Poems in Memory of Julia Casterton

1. A City Meadow

A butterfly flits into our meadow of wild
flowers, swishes her scarf over her shoulder,
asks me to introduce myself –
And are you married?
I explain my wife has died. *Oh,*
she says, *we've got a widower.*

After I've read my poem, she turns
like a sonnet,
alights on a familiar phrase, and says
If you can say that in a different way Peter,
please let me know. It may be rather difficult
but well worth trying. Then she's gone,

fluttering off, hovers over a cowslip,
Hello Helen, what have you been writing?

2. Conjuring Tricks

I'm rehearsing my sleight of hand,
craft of the illusionist

when reason translates to the spiritual
with the tumble of words

to the next line and everyone
gets excited, exclaiming

ooh and *ah. How is that done?*
It's when I say 'abracadabra'

reach into a top hat
for a rainbow of bunting

flapping in predictable rhythms,
wave my wand and they become

lines of light and art.
Then the magician in me

opens his palms and out flutter
twenty doves (from Finisterre of course)

into the air, your years of inspiration,
to fly in couplets round the page

sensual and eloquent
beautifully lineated.

3. Address Book

Going through my address book
the pencil hovers at Cable Street
with its Whitechapel memories
of Huguenots, Jews, Bangladeshis.

You were always drawn to the newly
arrived, gave most attention
to their hesitant voices, with plenty
left for the more settled.

Even if I cross you out, you're indelible.

III

NO SCHOOL TIE

Life in the Jungle

Nuns sweep me into Kindergarten; a left-handed
five-year-old who writes 2 back to front soon feels

the scorch from their glares. Next the hothouse:
peaked cap and red look-at-me blazer. Here I learn

to spell *anxiety*. At nine, I'm sent to the jungle,
swelter on a train shunting from Victoria.

Have I forgotten my torch? Every three weeks
Mother and Father hack through the undergrowth,

lunch at the Grand Brighton, breast of chicken,
chips and salad cream – all I would eat.

Then a game of table tennis, a handful of pennies
for the West Pier slot machines, the journey back –

car and homesickness welling inside me. At night
I hug my bear, blue fur on my face till I fade into

sleep. Next morning I put him under the pillow.
Now I'm right-handed, can write 2 correctly.

I'm trekking back.

Walking Home from School

A humanity of coal horse stands in our street.
His old sack nosebag hangs from a mouth full
of chomp, jaws grinding in slow circles.

I don't touch his dirty neck, far too high to reach,
can stroke a leg, but when he shuffles, lifts
a hoof to mark his spot, I back away. The horse

looks like a Fred or Ted. Is it his easy pull-and-tug
nature, or outcast face making me stare?
A pile of dung steams the ground; my schoolboy

laughter runs me home, away from the jangling
harness, towards tea and times tables.

Boxing Exhibition

We're in the wings, black plimsolls tied
tightly. Schoolboy gladiators Lance and I
have a plan. He'll land three punches
hard to my head. I'll return them.
We'll skip round, striking each other in turn.

Into the ring and the trench of our stomachs.
The lights are bright. The bell bongs,
the hall looks up, an assembly
of baying parents.

Now we're bouncing about, gloves
shield our faces. I take three punches,
he throws a fourth, *Bang,*
then a fifth, *Bang.* Now
I know Lance can't count.

We carry on beating each other
till the three-minute bell goes.

Mother and Father are out there –
somewhere.

Victoria Station

Young boys tread water
trying not to go under.

In we push, past the barrier,
to the slam of carriage doors,

worse than the dread of boxing
worse than arithmetic.

Hands held tight
saying goodbye –

I climb amongst the rabbits,
tuck boxes and other nine-year-olds.

What's your name?
Where do you live?

Mother waits on the platform smiling.
The window is drawn down –

We don't talk.
I can't talk.

A hiss of steam lets off.
No one has drowned.

There's a jolt as the train pulls me
backwards to Eastbourne.

The smile on Mother's face
slowly disappears.

Queueing for Supper

It hasn't taken long for my dormitory to learn
how to dream of Sunday roast at home –

bread and dripping at the head
of a queue of dressing gowns. I plunge

the knife into the dish of chipped white
enamel, spread a thick slice to the crust's

edge. It tastes like meat. I search
for the gravy marbling, mostly at the bottom,

the darker scrapings the other boys
have gone for. Fat chance.

'Are You Still Blocked Dear?'

Mother has given me my own
little bottle of Dulcolax.
No more headaches or strained
muscles, just regular, until Matron
confiscates my toilet lifeline.

Once a week I'm an undercover agent
in pyjamas, stealing
secrets from the enemy. I creep
down, open the dispensary, find
the yellow pills, take
one for today and a spare.

Then Mother gives me another bottle;
she's a double agent
slipping me more secrets when she visits;
but the top comes off on a cross-country run,
leaving a trail through a field of cows.

Every time I see a cowpat, I feel sorry.

Taking a Shower for the First Time

We shuffle towards Matron's stiff uniform.
No talking in the showers.
Make sure you get clean.

Baths are twice a week. Mother had said
I might also want a strip wash,
didn't mention showers,
or the mystical locker rooms
where towels are held tight on nakedness.

Six baths side by side, mud swirling
down the plugholes.
Towels are dropped.
I take a side-squint
at the others. Gosh he's big.
Oh, he's small –

We climb in.
I'm washing away Sussex,
hard-fought-for mud, streaking
in victory.
Then dress, check the board for homework.
Oh balls, it's maths.

On Being Called to the Head

Two years after me, twin sister Sue is sent
to boarding school, goes eagerly to enjoy

Set times for prep and games. But Mother,
wanting to love a child at home again, and making

plans with Father, is surprised by more twins, another
boy and girl. Called to see the Head, I stand to hear

this skilful news, and say, with excruciating niceness,
'This is the happiest day of my life.'

As adults, we asked Father many times how
he did this trick of having twins, and would he

like to try once more for luck? He always
said with a smile, *Go and ask your mother.*

Growing Carrots

A London boy is pulling up carrots. A rabbit's
misted eyes protrude as breath whispers away.

Brown brogues on the earth. Then a golf club
swishing through the air. I look up into Sir's

nostrils – amongst ourselves, we call him Corporal.
'There's a rabbit here Sir.' His club

rolls the rabbit to the grass's edge.
He stands astride her as if driving off

from the first tee, steadies himself, swings,
strikes her into the fairway of the cricket pitch.

He wipes the club's head on the grass.
Best thing for it he says, strolling back to school.

I follow, forget my carrots lying in neat piles.

Goodnight in the Jungle

A prefect-gorilla from the high ground
swings through before lights out.

Sometimes, to go to sleep with, we'll get
a few grunts, a thump on the arm

to keep us quiet. As he moves off
we listen to the faraway rustle of branches.

Out come our torches, a shandy,
and a cigarette shared between six.

Erotic Vision

Six of us bus to Rye. Climb
the country lanes, engine juddering
as if the string might snap. Then down
to the cobbled town, into the cinema,
a scramble to watch Dr No and gawp
at Ursula Andress in white bikini,
our eyes bursting at her curves as she comes
towards our front row seats
out of the Caribbean. We laugh

into the six o'clock night, queue
for newspapered chips – what
is a Martini shaken not stirred?
Does Sir drink them, maybe?
Matron wouldn't, no Matron wouldn't.
What about when Bond bites
the poison from her foot?
That must have hurt. And always

the image of Ursula *Undress*
as we now call her. Oh,
how we'll boast to the others,
and sealed in our heads forever
that bikini,
and for me an embedded
love of chip shops.

Bath Time Butterflies

A butterfly comes to rest,
level with my eyes, on the edge of the bath.

She's a Painted Lady – I'd been praying
to see one soon – and her wings quiver

in the steamy heat of the water.
She flits to my stomach, settles between

my thighs. Then others fly in,
Red Admirals, Large Whites, more Painted Ladies,

a mass of wings fanning the glow
in a swirl of colour, till their flutter

giddies me in a breathless rainbow rush
and they're flying to another fourteen-year-old.

It was better than scoring a penalty,
even Mother sending money.

I tell myself I'll give up the butterflies
when I've seen them ten times,

but after I get to double figures, I lose count

Imagining Matron

Bossy-buxom, a mix of Hattie Jacques
and Rosa Kleb, her shoe-tips deadly,
was what I got in the sick bay. What

I wanted was an Anna from Denmark,
who came from her parents' little farm in Jutland
and desperately wanted to meet well-behaved

sixteen-year-old English boys. She'd look after us,
come and sit on the edge of my bed in her nightdress,
dab my brow fevered with excitement, and ask

with a smile *Is there anything else I can do?*
But when I'd reach to touch a pale shoulder
and, accidentally, her breast, just at the point

of touching she'd dissolve, go to someone
like Harris, the captain of football.

Sex Education

Albert the gardener talked
about fertilizer. The vicar went pale.
Miss Compton became agitated, told us
to go away. The Head didn't want
to get involved, nor did his wife.
The Major had no idea. Biology

was all frogspawn. So Sex meant
asking each other questions:
What does it feel like?
Do you really do that?
Don't girls mind?

We had a chat-up line for next time
we met a girl. It seemed unfair
to try my sister's girlfriends,
but I had a go and nodded
a sort of leering smile. Words
tumbled in clumsy heaps,
redness staining my face.

When my daughter went to university
I asked if I needed to tell her anything.
No thank you Dad she said.
Well, I thought, that's her sorted.

Fielding My Imagination

Anywhere else makes me dream –
I ask to go in the slips – no
time to think of home,
what I'll do with a first girlfriend.

This is where I concentrate,
hunched over knees for a catch
edged off the bat. Thoughts
of the ball hitting my head

keep me awake. Sometimes I lose
attention, think about Mother's
lamb chops, the latest issue
of Health and Efficiency

hidden deep under my pal's mattress
and how I'm going to get hold of it.
Then there's the thwack of the ball.
Everyone's running. It's been struck

to the boundary (my head's
still out there) but now it arcs
back to the stumps. Holdsworth
has his wicketkeeper's gloves open

and hopeful. He looks up, sways
a little. The ball paints the sky.
I hear myself say, 'Doesn't it look red
against the blue?' It drops towards me.

Airfix

I always wanted to be a tail gunner
but the diagram was too difficult
or a piece went missing. Now the fuselage
clips into place, then the wings. Pots of paint
are empty, transfers stuck on. We climb in.

Hamish crosses himself, stubs
a cigarette, grins. The runway rolls.
We mop our faces. I hum 'Run Rabbit Run'
and the undercarriage bumps up. We fly
over the Dutch coast to the Ruhr. I'm looking

for the enemy, then flak bursts around us,
the bombs are away and the whole
thing just goes – it was like…
water sweeping, everything.

Bullets pierce the Lancaster. Whines
from a Messerschmitt screech through us –
a fire spits into life.
Out, out. Then we're swinging
down the sky. Our plane,
a roar of flame, spins past.

Hamish raises a thumb. The bell rings
for dinner. A fighter flies towards us,
its riddle of bullets tear
into me. I crash-land the Lancaster
inside my desk, join the queue.

Announcement

It's dinner and the Head comes in.

Please stand, boys. I have to tell you
President Kennedy has been shot.

We sit down and get on with our meal:
cottage pie and, to follow, hot chocolate
sponge and sauce. Someone asks,

Who's President Kennedy?
He's given a kick.

Being Different

A boy was a boy if he scored goals –
or didn't try too hard in class.

Most couldn't see it, but to one
I was a bloody Jew.

He crouched in the low light,
always there, siphoning off

my confidence into his tank.
In a quiet Sunday corridor

he got me. We rolled on the floor,
but when I told him I'd kill him

it was over. That afternoon I went
to Drama, auditioned for

the Bloody Sergeant in Scene One.

Religious Studies

The other boys are at church.
I study for my bar mitzvah
in the office, eyes closing
over my correspondence course,
feet up on his desk, playing
at being headmaster.

I like his letters arranged
in tidy thoughts, the blotter ink-stained
with reports to parents, the view
of the croquet lawn, and I'm thinking:

The mallets have been left out.
Shall I hide them for afterwards?
Who will I play with, maybe Holdsworth?
I'm a bit hungry and, gosh
who's that coming downstairs?

I whisk my feet off the desk,
push my hair into place – *Hello
Phillips. How are you getting on?*
'All right, thank you Sir.
How are you?'

Sherry with the Deputy Head

Head Boy's duty, or treat?
Friday evening before dinner.
Hello Peter, how are you?
'My maths is coming along, Sir,
and I beat Mr Hobbs at table tennis.'

But you told me that last week.
Then he pours two large glasses,
pale and dry. I sip mine,
try to think what to say.
'Yes Sir, but nothing has happened since then.'

Make sure it does next week, he says.

Biking My Way Through Maths

Father said *You must make sure you get*
maths O level, you'll need that later in life.

I said, to myself, 'I will do well in maths
to thank you for the Bike.' Bike emboldened me.

On Saturday and Sunday afternoons I battled
with angles, equations, fractions. Exam day

wasn't a straight knockout. Maths was tough,
I was weary. But Bike, in all its chrome

and greenness, was in my corner, wiping
a bloody nose, towel on handlebar. Next term,

just to make sure, I fought Maths again –
this time at a girls' school. They wore brown

uniforms with red tops. There I was with thirty
robins and me in their nest. And Bike?

I left him in the shed for the juniors.

No School Tie

There's no school tie to open doors,
just a green cravat
from Father, a bit swish
as I puff it up round my neck
before the interview.

Sitting cross-legged on the desk
there'll be the prefect-gorilla from my jungle days,
a bunch of bananas on his lap.
Love the green scarf Phillips,
green's a good colour round here.
Come in. Do you still have nits?

Talking up life in equatorial Canary Wharf,
he'll swing to and fro on his high-backed chair.
Then he'll swivel round,
When can you start?

'But don't you want to ask
about my experience?'
No need for that, just make sure
you're hunting in my pack.
'By the way… what should I call you?'
Bunny, of course –
but Sir in front of the others.

He'll raise a furry fist, gently press
his knuckles to the top of my arm,
grin as he opens the door.

The Bar, Windsor Hotel, Melbourne

There he is, bent forward, leaning
into our reunion, ox-frame lumbering
down the cricket pitch corridor
as we come in from the boundary.

Hello mate he says, and when we shake hands,
I feel the weight of friendship
in his clasp. We're back forty-five years,
striplings, thin, and anxious
for catches, first kisses and more.

No parents to pay for lunch
or high tea; just buying each other beers
one after another,
and a Chinese meal in town.

Next day there's a barbecue at his place
(competing with dog for chops and sausages),
plenty of drink.

And at the end of the final day,
heads a little low
as we walk in from the wicket,
See you mate he says.

About the Author

Peter Phillips is a London poet. His three previous collections, all published by Hearing Eye, were:

Wide Skies, Salt and Best Bitter, 2005
Looking For You, 2001
Frayed At The Edges (pamphlet), 1997

For more about this author online see his pages:
on the *poetry pf* website www.poetrypf.co.uk
and on www.wardwoodpublishing.co.uk